# HILLARY CLINTON

# Table of Contents

Introduction

Chapter 1: Birth and Childhood

Chapter 2: College Years

Chapter 3: Law School and More

Chapter 4: Marrying Bill

Chapter 5: Life as a Lawyer

Chapter 6: In the Governor's Mansion

Chapter 7: Raising Chelsea

Chapter 8: Campaigning for Bill's Presidency

Chapter 9: First Lady and West Wing Insider

Chapter 10: Health Care Task Force

Chapter 11: Speaking Out for Women's Rights

Chapter 12: Whitewater Investigation

Chapter 13: Writings

Chapter 14: U.S. Senator

Chapter 15: First Presidential Campaign

Chapter 16: Secretary of State

Chapter 17: Benghazi

Chapter 18: Second Presidential Campaign

Conclusion

# Introduction

Hillary Clinton is a strong and resilient woman with her own opinions. Not content to stay on the sidelines as a demure First Lady, she tackled one of the most challenging tasks the United States government has faced as she worked toward a national health care plan. She had an office in the West Wing, a first among First Ladies. She was the first to host a White House webcast and the first to run for an elected office. Not since Eleanor Roosevelt took the position of First Lady has anyone redefined the role so profoundly.

As the first female U.S. Senator for New York, Clinton refused to use her former First Lady status to try to gain special privileges or attention. She developed relationships with both Republicans and Democrats in Congress and then went on to serve on several Senate Committees. As Secretary of State, she dealt with severe world crises as well as her regular State Department duties.

Although her name has been associated with a wide range of controversies and scandals, her supporters would say that Hillary Clinton has never backed away from her responsibilities. From the Monika Lewinsky debacle to allegations of her blame for the Benghazi terrorist attack to her alleged misuse of personal emails to conduct government business, Hillary has withstood the pressure and kept moving forward. Some might allege that she has made poor choices, but there can be no doubt that she has remained steadfast in the face of criticism.

Yet, the question remains for many Americans, and indeed for politically-minded people around the world, who is Hillary Clinton? Is she someone who can be trusted to lead a democracy as vast as the United States? Where will the United States be in four years if she is elected president in 2016?

This book seeks to provide a brief introduction to Hillary Clinton and her extraordinary life - starting from the very beginning. The right to vote is a precious thing, and a right that not all people in the world have been granted, even now. We hope this book will provide a clearer picture of this presidential candidate.

# Chapter 1

# Birth and Childhood

On October 26, 1947, just over two years after the end of World War II, Hillary Diane Rodham was born in Chicago, Illinois. Her father was Hugh Ellsworth Rodham, a small businessman. Her mother, Dorothy Emma Howell, worked to provide a comfortable and stable home for the family. Two sons, Hugh and Tony, were born into the family in 1950 and 1954.

Hugh Rodham was a strict – some would say harsh – parent. He expected Hillary to toe the line and was reportedly often sarcastic to her and her brothers when they failed to live up to his expectations. Yet, he taught Hillary about business and how to manage money. He also raised her to be a fierce competitor and a strong woman. He may have been cruel at times, but he wanted his daughter to have the opportunity to put her talents to good use.

Dorothy, Hillary's mother, always wanted her to succeed in life on her own merits in any career field she chose. In the years since, Hillary has spoken of her mother as one of the primary inspirations in her life. Although Dorothy was a homemaker, she was active in the community and truly cared about other people less fortunate. Dorothy may not have had a big, fancy career, but she wanted her daughter to be able to pursue any interest, regardless of whether it was a traditionally male industry or not.

Hillary was a good student, liked by both teachers and students at her Park Ridge elementary school. She was an athlete, participating in swimming and baseball. She attended Brownies and Girl Scouts, an organization she would later head as its honorary president in her role as the First Lady. Young Hillary wanted to be an astronaut at one point, and even wrote a letter to NASA requesting information about how to get into the program. NASA wrote a response saying that no females were being accepted.

At Maine East High School, Hillary was vice president of her student council in her junior year. She ran for president of the student council her senior year but lost – not surprising in a culture where girls were secretaries and guys were presidents. She continued to be an outstanding student, as is evident by her membership in the National Honor Society. In 1965, at Maine South High School, Hillary was near the top of her class, graduating in the top 5%.

Hillary worked as a young student, babysitting when not in school, often for children of migrant workers. During her high school years, she organized food drives to help the needy. Her high school history teacher and Methodist youth leader inspired her and encouraged her to participate in the political process. Her youth leader took her to listen to a speech by Reverend Martin Luther King, Jr., and she met him briefly. At the age of 13, Hillary was involved in canvassing Southside Chicago after the close 1960 election. She was active in the Young Republican organization and even campaigned for Barry Goldwater in 1964. In 1965, Hillary enrolled in Wellesley College to major in political science and psychology.

# Chapter 2

# College Years

Although her parents raised her to consider herself equally competitive with both genders, Hillary Rodham chose to enroll in Wellesley, an all-female school near Boston. To those who are unfamiliar with all women's colleges, this might seem the easy way out for such a strong-minded student.

However, as studies show, even the most vocal women students speak less in a co-ed institution than in a single-sex school. Since gender is not a factor in the classroom, students are not pigeonholed into traditionally male occupations. Women are encouraged to seek the profession that speaks to them and gives them opportunities to use their own intellectual gifts.

In her freshman year, Hillary was already the president of the Young Republicans at her college. However, inspired by the building anti-war sentiment in the U.S. and the growing civil rights movement, Hillary began to change her views. Although she still considered herself conservatively-minded, she told her youth leader she had realized her heart was liberal. Yet, far from being anti-establishment, she saw her way forward as a leader, helping to change the system from the inside.

As she had during her earlier years, Hillary found candidates to support and worked hard to help them win. She favored Eugene McCarthy as the presidential nominee during her junior year. That year, she also served as president of the Wellesley College Government Association.

After civil rights leader Martin Luther King, Jr. was assassinated, she organized a strike. She also reached out to black students and faculty, encouraging them to become a part of the Wellesley College community.

Professor Alan Schechter sent her to the House Republican Conference to work as an intern. She was chosen to help with Nelson Rockefeller win the Republican nomination for President. However, once at the convention, she was disillusioned when she heard the subtle but definite trend toward racism from the Republican Party. By the time her internship had concluded, she had decided that the Democratic Party was the one that would help her advance her goals.

During the summer between her junior and senior years at Wellesley, Rodham met Saul Alinsky, a radical activist and community organizer. Alinsky worked and wrote to bring power to the have-nots by taking power away from those who had it. He later contributed his time to help Rodham understand his views and methods so she could write her senior thesis on him. She wrote with deep admiration for his motives while criticizing the methods he chose to change the world.

Hillary Rodham graduated from college in 1969. She gave a commencement speech that was the first to come from a student in that institution. That speech, which criticized the Republican U.S. Senator Edward Brooke who had just spoken before her, garnered her a 7-minute standing ovation and inspired *Life* magazine to publish an article about her. She was also a hit on TV shows and newspapers in several states.

Hillary spent the summer following graduation in Alaska, working at various jobs to earn her living expenses and save for graduate school. After she complained of conditions at a salmon processing factory where she worked, her employment was terminated. However, the experience would add to her growing commitment to creating positive change.

# Chapter 3

# Law School and More

As Hillary Rodham made plans to attend law school, Saul Alinsky told her that she could not change anything by becoming a lawyer. She, however, adamantly disagreed. She began her law studies at Yale Law School in 1969, the next fall after her graduation from Wellesley.

Becoming a lawyer would allow her opportunities to follow her ideals by working within the system to effect social change, and perhaps that was her primary motivation for choosing the profession. Or, she might have already seen that it was a stepping stone to a political position in which she would have more power to help people. Whatever the reason, she excelled as a student, as always.

At Yale, Rodham became friends with many of the anti-establishment leaders on campus. Then, rather than working at the *Yale Law Journal,* she chose instead to sit on join the editorial board of *The Yale Review of Law and Social Action*.

At the time Rodham was working on that publication, the trial of seven Black Panthers accused of killing another Black Panther was going on. She attended court to observe the workings of the legal system in this racially-charged trial. If there were any civil rights violations during the trial, she was to report them to the ACLU. And, despite what some would consider her bent towards radicalism, the truth is that Hillary Rodham believed in working through the system. It was their ideals she valued, not their tactics.

On several notable occasions at Yale, Rodham played an intermediary role between factions. During discussions among students, she often injected her sense of balance and practicality. And, when the International Law Library was set on fire, Hillary grabbed buckets of water and helped put it out. Shortly afterward, she sat at the front of a large lecture hall, helping protestors and faculty understand each other as they clashed on the issues of the times.

Hillary began working on one of her lifetime goals while at Yale by working at the school's

Child Study Center. She served as a lawyer for children who had been abused. She worked as a pro bono lawyer for the poor, as well, and received a grant to work on a Washington Research Project, headed by Marian Wright Edelman. Her task there was to work with Senator Walter Mondale on his Subcommittee on Migratory Labor.

Hillary has said that Connecticut U.S. Senate candidate Joseph Duffey gave her the first real job she ever had in politics, even though she had been volunteering her services to political campaigns for years before.

In 1971, Rodham started her internship in the law at the legal firm of Treuhaft, Walker, and Burnstein. The firm was famous for its support of civil rights activists and radicals. Rodham then went on to graduate from Yale Law School with a Juris Doctor degree in 1973.

Afterward, she continued her studies, learning even more about children's rights and medical care. This experience would help fuel her interest in causes relating to children – information and views she would later use to compose some of the most influential scholarly articles on the subject. However, meanwhile, she

had developed another interest. His name was
William Jefferson Clinton.

# Chapter 4

# Marrying Bill

As Hillary Rodham Clinton tells the story, it was she who first approached Bill Clinton. The two had been exchanging glances at the library. After a while, Hillary went to him and told him that if they were going to continue looking at each other, they had better get to know each other. Her husband has agreed with this story, saying he was so stunned he even forgot his name for a moment. Shortly afterward, they began dating.

When Hillary was interning with Treuhaft, Walker, and Burnstein in California, Bill dropped his summer plans to be with her there. They moved together back to New Haven and continued pursuing their law degrees. They worked together in Texas the next summer, campaigning for presidential candidate George McGovern. McGovern's bid for the presidency failed, but the Rodham-Clinton relationship was still going strong. Hillary moved to Arkansas to join the future president.

When Hillary graduated from Yale Law School, she and Bill took a trip to Europe. He proposed to her there. Rodham refused him at that time, concerned that their marriage would change the path she was determined to follow. However, as time would tell, their union ultimately helped her gain recognition for her contributions to the country. Bill proposed many times, but Hillary refused to accept until she was sure of her answer.

Bill finally won her over by buying a home that he insisted the two of them must share. It was a house Hillary had seen and admired on the way to the airport as she left to visit friends and begin a job search. When she returned, Bill brought her to the house he had bought and proposed once more. This time, she agreed to marry him.

Hillary Rodham and Bill Clinton tied the knot in that very same home in Fayetteville, Arkansas on October 11, 1975. The ceremony was small, with only 15 friends and family members attending. When the Methodist minister and his wife concluded the ceremony, Bill and Hillary hosted a wedding reception in their backyard, where several hundred guests joined them.

Hillary retained her maiden name for professional reasons. She wanted to stay a Rodham to remind herself and others that she was still an individual, responsible for her own decisions and accomplishments. Both Bill's and Hillary's mothers were unhappy about the decision, but Hillary was adamant that it was the right choice.

The newlyweds only lived in that house for a little while before moving to the Arkansas capital of Little Rock. Hillary speaks of the little house fondly, perhaps remembering a more innocent time in their relationship.

Later on, the marriage would suffer as allegations about Bill having affairs with various other women arose. However, Hillary stayed with Bill through the accusations and even his admitted indiscretions. While her detractors continue to say that her public response was too generous, her supporters suggest that the incidents involved display her strength in difficult situations.

Yet, the scandals were only a small part of their relationship. They have lived and worked together most of the time since their marriage, tackling difficult issues facing the country while raising their only child, Chelsea, and seeing her mature into a wise and intelligent woman. But, Hillary had many tasks to work on before Chelsea made her appearance. Her first stop was the Rose Law Firm.

# Chapter 5

# Life as a Lawyer

Before Rodham concluded her postgraduate studies, she worked as a consultant to the Carnegie Council on Children. In 1974, she assisted with impeachment research regarding the Watergate scandal as an advisor to the House Committee on the Judiciary.

Afterward, when Hillary went to Fayetteville, Arkansas to follow Bill, she knew she was limiting her career potential, if only for a while. However, there were opportunities in her new home. She took a position on the faculty of the University of Arkansas, Fayetteville, School of Law. She was known as a professor who demanded much of her students.

While working as a professor in Arkansas, Rodham also took on the job of director for the school's new legal aid clinic. She was appalled when she had to defend a man who raped a 12-year-old girl. Although she provided him with an outstanding legal defense, as was her responsibility, she hated every minute of it and, afterward, helped found a rape crisis center in Fayetteville.

When Bill Clinton became the Arkansas Attorney General in 1976, the couple moved to Little Rock. By the next year, Rodham was working at the prestigious Rose Law Firm. There, Hillary spent little time in court but was an advisor on patent law and intellectual property rights. She also followed her heart by working pro bono advocating for children.

The year 1977 was an important one, as Rodham helped found the Arkansas Advocates for Children and Families. Then, too, she served on the board of the Legal Services Corporation. From 1978 to 1980, she was the chairperson of the board and continued on the board until 1981. While she was chairperson, she expanded the funding for the corporation and won a victory as she fought against Reagan's agenda of cutting funding for the organization.

Hillary Rodham became First Lady of Arkansas when Bill Clinton became governor of that state in 1979. Hillary continued at the Rose Law Firm, where she was made a full partner – the first female in that firm to hold the position.

Hillary was also investing at that time, trying to supplement the family income. She turned $1,000 into $100,000 by trading in cattle futures. Although that investment worked out well, another venture would haunt the couple far into the future. It was at this time that they invested in the Whitewater Development Corporation.

Yet, Whitewater may have seemed like a minor detail in their lives. Bill had a state to lead, and Hillary's position as First Lady put her in a leadership role as well. They moved to the governor's mansion to begin fulfilling their duties.

# Chapter 6

# In the Governor's Mansion

Hillary Rodham Clinton served as First Lady of Arkansas during Bill Clinton's two terms as governor, from 1979 to 1981 and from 1983 to 1992. In this role, she served the public in various significant ways and, of course, met the social obligations the position demanded of her. At the same time, she continued to work at the Rose Law Firm.

President Clinton assigned her to the chair of the Arkansas Educational Standards Committee. In this role, she worked towards raising teacher wages while supporting mandatory testing of the teachers' abilities.

She also pushed for the state to develop their first curricular standards. Some people criticize her efforts on the committee, saying that the tests she backed caused many teachers to fail until the standards were lowered. Yet, the Arkansas schools did improve, and Hillary was seen as one of the stronger forces behind the change.

Hillary held three positions during this time that contributed to her goal of serving young people and their parents. She worked with the Arkansas Advocates for Children and Families.

She also continued to provide help for abused children in her role with the Arkansas Children's Hospital Legal Services. Finally, she kept working for the Children's Defense Fund to work towards legislation that would benefit children. And, from 1987 to 1991, she was the chairperson for the American Bar Association's Commission on Women in the Profession.

While managing her professional legal duties and keeping up with her duties as First Lady of Arkansas, Rodham Clinton also served on the boards of several large retail corporations, including TCBY, Lefarge, and Walmart.

Some people have criticized her for being associated with Walmart, a retail giant that many consider to be an evil corporation. They suggest that she should have fought harder against what they consider some of the most unfair practices in the business. However, Hillary was instrumental in Walmart's decision to adopt nondiscriminatory hiring practices.

Rodham took on one other personal and profoundly meaningful role when she was living in the Arkansas governor's mansion: she became a mother.

# Chapter 7

# Raising Chelsea

On February 27, 1980, Chelsea Victoria Clinton came into the world by cesarean birth. Bill and Hillary had visited the Chelsea area of London two years before, and after Bill heard Joni Mitchell's "Chelsea Morning," he suggested they choose that name for their daughter if they should ever have one.

When Bill was on the campaign trail to win his second term as governor of Arkansas, the Clintons took two-year-old Chelsea with them.

Hillary and Bill sent Chelsea to public schools in Little Rock for her elementary and junior high school education. Jacqueline Kennedy Onassis and Margaret Truman had advised Hillary that too much media coverage was a difficult proposition for a young child suddenly thrust into the limelight by her parents' achievements. So, Hillary encouraged Chelsea to go to a private school for her high school education to limit her exposure in the media.

Hillary was a busy professional, but she always made time to be a mother to Chelsea. At the 2016 Democratic National Convention, Chelsea spoke fondly of her childhood and her mother's role in it. Chelsea stated that Hillary attended her soccer and softball games as well as her piano and dance recitals.

Mealtime conversations always started out focusing on Chelsea's schoolwork before going on to news of what her parents were doing. And, when Hillary was away, she left notes for young Chelsea to read every day in her absence.

During that convention speech, Chelsea referred to another gift she got from her mother. It was the same gift Hillary's mother had given to her. It was an awareness of and commitment to public service done for the sake of serving others rather than for any fame or political gain. Chelsea continued by telling stories of how her mother took time to give needy mothers personal attention before working behind these scenes to create a way for the mothers to solve their problems.

Hillary Rodham Clinton was named as Arkansas Woman of the Year in 1983 and, perhaps even more meaningful in some ways, as Arkansas Mother of the Year in 1984. She continues to have a profound effect on Chelsea's children as their doting grandmother. And, Chelsea has always been proud of her mother and grateful for the way her mother raised her.

There were times when controversies surrounding Hillary or Bill caused young Chelsea a certain degree of discomfort. However, she always knew that they loved her, and she continued to support them throughout every ordeal and still does today. She has been a part of her parents' political lives for all of hers, so she understands better than anyone how to make the best of difficult situations. Her first significant exposure to politics came when she was very young, as she joined her parents on a tour of Arkansas to boost Bill's chances to regain the governorship.

That trip would be an important one for Hillary, too, as she put her campaign experience to work supporting her husband's career while honing political skills she had already developed. By the time Bill was ready to campaign for the presidency, Hillary was more than prepared.

# Chapter 8

# Campaigning for Bill's Presidency

Remember that up to 1992, when Bill Clinton ran for President of the United States for the first time, Hillary had already had a very successful career and had become extremely influential in her profession, and in Arkansas in general. No one who had come in any significant contact with her could have possibly imagined that she was riding on Bill's coattails.

However, Bill's presidential campaign was the first time massive numbers of people outside their state and profession had ever heard of her. Most everyday people at that time did not get to meet her on her terms, but only in relation to Bill's career. This fact may have skewed their perception of her, at least for a time.

During his run for president, it was alleged that Bill Clinton had had an affair with Gennifer

Flowers, a lounge singer from Clinton's home state. The media ran with the story, and soon the alleged affair became household news.

To combat the negative press, Hillary and Bill appeared together on *60 Minutes* to discuss the allegations. While Bill maintained that no affair ever happened, he did say that he had been the cause of pain within his marriage.

Hillary spoke as well during the broadcast, although she may have regretted the words she chose. When she used a wordplay on the Tammy Wynette classic song "Stand by Your Man," she managed to insult both country music fans and homemakers. Tammy Wynette defended herself in a letter to Hillary. Hillary apologized quickly, saying that the words were not well-chosen.

After that, the noise died down. Her detractors still used her decision to stay with Bill, regardless of any allegations of affairs, to make the point that a real feminist would have left him. However, others say that the pair shared an intellectual and emotional bond that was deeper than any affairs could have possibly been. At any rate, the Clintons continued to stand together, and it was on with the political race.

Bill Clinton pointed out his wife's accomplishments and promised the American people that, in voting for him, they would get the benefit of her contributions to the government as well. With Hillary's experience, education, and talent, that was a more powerful promise than many viewers and readers could fully comprehend. Both as First Lady and later on, Hillary Rodham Clinton worked hard within the system, just as she had planned to do long before she met Bill.

After an article in The American Spectator compared Hillary to Lady Macbeth, other publications ran similar articles. Yet, the idea that Hillary Rodham needed a man to exert influence in the world made little sense to those who had seen what she accomplished on her own. And, even though there were conservatives who criticized Hillary and described her past ideological and ethical choices as less than wholesome, it seems that there were more who believed she would make an admirable First Lady. After all, they knew she would hold that position if Bill succeeded, and enough cast their votes in his favor that Bill Clinton won the election.

Hillary saw the opportunities that lay ahead in her new role as First Lady. Bill had plans for her, too. Over the next eight years, the American people would see a new kind of First Couple in the White House, a couple where both had the educational and professional backgrounds to make the most of those opportunities that came along.

# Chapter 9

# First Lady and West Wing Insider

During his campaign, Bill Clinton had promised a team approach to the presidency. Before he could do that, though, he had to convince the public that he was truly in charge of the country. As Hillary took on a more significant role in the government than First Ladies typically had before, her influence was felt and possibly exaggerated by the media.

The truth is that Hillary did not run the country. Yet, she did advise the president, much as any advisor would. When a cabinet member was to be chosen, Bill often would go to Hillary's West Wing office and discuss the matter with her.

Yet, it was the president who made the decisions. Hillary merely provided input based on her years of experience and relying on her own political network to learn more about the issues and people involved.

Early in Bill Clinton's first term, he had a problem finding an Attorney General. His first choice turned out to have hired an illegal alien as a housekeeper, causing controversy about whether a law-breaker such as she could possibly be an acceptable choice. During the "Nanny-Gate" incident, Hillary talked to Bill about other possibilities.

Yet again, he made the final decision – against her suggestion – when he was with other advisors. Still, Hillary did exert a more considerable influence than most other First Ladies have in the past as Bill put her talents and network to good use.

Hillary Rodham Clinton's days as First Lady were extraordinarily busy. She tended to her ceremonial duties, supported her only child's activities, and made changes to the White House living quarters.

She made a policy of no smoking in the White House complex and ensured that plenty of fruits and vegetables were available at meals and for snacks. And, she juggled these responsibilities in the same way many working mothers did at that time.

While some people, especially conservatives, felt that Hillary had too much power, many others looked up to her as a role model. After all, she worked hard, divided her time between many different responsibilities and interests, and seemed to be thriving through every ordeal.

When the President appointed her to lead the task force on health care, Hillary was in her element as usual. She brought an enormous amount of energy and intelligence to the project, even though it was largely an uphill battle. She tackled the problem with the nation's health care system by thinking in logical and practical ways. It would prove to be one of her toughest challenges.

# Chapter 10

# Health Care Task Force

One of the first things Bill Clinton did as President in 1993 was to appoint Hillary Rodham Clinton as the head of a new Task Force on National Health Care Reform. Hillary had been successful in turning around the Arkansas education system and had always been concerned about health, so she must have been a natural choice for the job.

After working on the problem, she supported a health care plan that would make businesses responsible for making health care available to their employees through HMOs. The plan would necessitate sweeping changes and government funding. Yet, it would have made it possible for anyone with a job to get health care.

Opponents dubbed the plan "Hillarycare," and even Democrats in Congress failed to support it. Rodham Clinton approached the job of getting the public's support for her plan in the same way she had approached getting Bill elected. She went on a tour, speaking to crowds around the country, even when the hostility against the plan was so apparent that she had to wear a bulletproof vest.

The plan failed in Congress without even enough support to force a vote. Hillary's approval ratings fell dramatically by the time the plan was officially defeated in September 1994. Rodham Clinton was discouraged and disconsolate for a time, but she did not drop out of public life or stop working towards her goals.

One health care problem she did help solve was getting guaranteed health care for children of the working poor. The CHIP plan, as it came to be known, has given children from families without enough money to buy health insurance medical coverage since it was passed in 1997.

Rodham Clinton had many interests in health care that she spoke out for and worked to achieve. She publicly supported and worked behind the scenes to encourage nationwide child immunization programs, mammograms for older women, and research for childhood asthma and prostate cancer. She was also worked towards finding out why Gulf War veterans were becoming ill, a cause that led to the discovery of Gulf War Syndrome.

Although not directly linked to health care, Rodham Clinton also had her say on welfare reform, which Bill Clinton was determined to see passed. The first two bills that the Republican-dominated Congress sent Bill were unhelpful for people getting off welfare. Hillary suggested he veto them, and he did. When a third bill was sent to Bill, Hillary accepted the plan and did not suggest that Bill should veto it, even though it was not her ideal plan.

When the main healthcare initiative failed, Hillary accepted a part of the blame, saying that if she had more political experience, it might have passed. Still, her work on this project gained her more experience, which she would later put to work on other projects.

# Chapter 11

# Speaking Out for Women's Rights

Hillary Clinton has always been a strong proponent of women's rights, both in the U.S. and around the world. When she helped found the Little Rock rape crisis center during her law school years, she was setting a pattern that she would follow for the rest of her career up to this point. That is, when she was exposed to a problem with women's issues, she worked to find practical solutions.

Some feminists have said that Clinton has missed opportunities to further the cause of equality for women. At the same time, some conservatives have called her a radical feminist and argued that she goes too far in her quest to make American life fairer for women. The truth is that Hillary Clinton has worked hard on these issues while being mindful of the way the government functions so she could create changes within the system.

Clinton's most defining moment as a feminist happened at the United Nations Fourth World Conference on Women that took place in Beijing, China in 1995. She went as a delegate to the conference, despite the reservations of many in Congress and even within the Clinton camp. She saw an opportunity to send a message about women to the nations of the world, and she seized that chance.

At the conference, she gave a speech that brought women from around the globe into the discussion of women's rights. During her forceful speech, she declared that "Women's rights are human rights," putting the issue into a new perspective for many women and bringing it to the attention of world leaders in a new way.

Since then, she has continued to fight for women's rights. She worked toward passage of the Family and Medical Leave Act, argued for more funding for childcare, and worked with others to begin the National Campaign to End Teen and Unplanned Pregnancy. Along the same lines as the latter, she has been a proponent of making emergency contraception available to women.

Planned Parenthood has become a controversial organization with conservatives suggesting its funding should be dropped. However, Hillary Clinton has continued to support Planned Parenthood in its mission to give women control over their own bodies and options for reproductive health.

Clinton has also lent her support to bills that promised to equalize women's pay and provide paid sick leave and parental leave to both women and men who work for the federal government. Hillary Clinton has said that if she becomes president, she will work even more to establish fair pay and fair opportunity for women.

Hillary Clinton has also discussed the rights of women in other countries. Although women in the U.S. have not yet reached equal status with men, the plight of women in many other countries is even worse. Clinton has spoken up for fair treatment of Afghani women and helped to set in motion an international campaign to encourage women's abilities to be a part of the political process in their respective countries.

Yet, even as Hillary Clinton worked so hard to help others, she was not free from troubles herself. A different sort of issue came back from the past to haunt her and Bill, starting at the time Bill was running for president for the first time. In 2016, many people forgot the details, but they still remember Whitewater.

# Chapter 12

# Whitewater Investigation

The Whitewater controversy surfaced just before
Bill Clinton won the presidency for the first term.
It was just one of the subjects covered in an
investigation led by Kenneth Starr into Bill and
Hillary Clinton's past. The investigation started in
1994, years after the Whitewater incident took
place. Although the aim was an impeachment of
President Bill Clinton, Hillary Clinton's activities
were also investigated.

Whitewater was a land development that Bill and
Hillary Clinton invested in in 1978. With Bill
working as Attorney General for Arkansas and
Hillary a low-level associate at the Rose Law
Firm, their combined earnings were reasonably
low, so they decided to invest in promising
ventures to increase their income.

The idea of the investment was that the Clintons,
along with Susan and James McDougal, would
purchase undeveloped land along the White

River in Arkansas and hold onto it until it increased in value. Then, they would sell it to a developer who could attract buyers with dreams of vacation homes in the Ozarks. But then, they began a development corporation to sell the lots themselves. The venture failed, and the Clintons lost a reported $40,000 in the deal.

James McDougal then decided to try his hand at banking and bought a savings and loan. McDougal made a series of fraudulent loans that resulted in his personal gain. The McDougals were found guilty of fraud, and the matter appeared to be settled.

However, since the Clintons were partners with the McDougals just prior to James buying the savings and loan, and because the Whitewater Corporation received some of the money from the loans, it was alleged that the Clintons were involved in fraudulent activities as well.

An investigation led by moderate Republican Robert B. Fiske, Jr. began in 1994. That same year, Fiske handed over the investigation to Kenneth Starr, a more conservative Republican. After questioning the Clintons and other witnesses for many hours and viewing documents related to the controversy, Starr filed an impeachment report in 1998. However, the Clintons were never found to be guilty of any wrongdoing in the Whitewater scandal.

Once the door was open to investigate the Clintons, many other issues surfaced. Travelgate involved the alleged illegal firing of White House travel coordinators, allegedly to make way for the Clintons selections to the posts. Filegate was the name used for an investigation into the alleged gathering of FBI files on notable Republicans. Another question was whether White House counsel Vince Foster had committed suicide or been murdered to cover up the Clintons' alleged wrongdoing. Vincent Foster's death was ruled to be a suicide after an exhaustive investigation.

And then, there was the alleged Monica Lewinsky affair. President Bill Clinton was accused of having an inappropriate sexual affair with White House intern Monica Lewinsky. This part of the investigation focused on the testimony of Bill Clinton, Monica Lewinsky, and others who were allegedly aware of their relationship. While Bill Clinton eventually agreed that he had had an inappropriate relationship with Lewinsky, he stopped short of admitting to a sexual affair.

In the end, the investigation left Hillary Clinton's reputation relatively unscathed, but Bill did not fare as well. Although Bill Clinton is remembered in a positive light for many of his presidential decisions, he is also remembered as the man who allegedly cheated on his wife. Through it all, Hillary Clinton maintained her dignity and minimized the drama of the incident significantly.

# Chapter 13

# Writings

Hillary Clinton's writing is best known for her book, *It Takes a Village*. That book sparked a controversy that enraged some parents who often had not even read more than the title. Some conservatives pointed to the title as a suggestion that parents' influence should be taken over by the state. However, other conservatives wrote positive reviews, saying that they agreed with the general premise of the book while disagreeing with some of the suggested programs.

While the book does cover many programs Hillary Clinton endorses to help children and families through government resources, it is mainly about how to raise children in the modern age. This is addressed to the parents who are doing the raising, as well as to those who have power and influence to change society to improve the lives of children.

Yet, many people do not realize that Hillary Rodham was writing important literature long before the 1996 publication of *It Takes a Village*. As every college student must, Hillary wrote many theses for her classes. During law school, she contributed scholarly articles to the *Yale Law Journal* and the *Harvard Educational Rev*iew. In these articles, she broke new ground by beginning from foundations laid by earlier experts to create comprehensive reports that tied together many different ideas that had not been looked at together before.

Her paper "Children Under the Law" is often cited and referred to by students, lawyers, and educators who want to share her insights and address issues related to children's legal rights. Her second major paper was "Children's Rights: A Legal Perspective." It is a review of earlier literature on the subject that does not draw its own conclusions except to establish a context for tying earlier ideas together.

In 2000, Hillary's book *An Invitation to the White House: A Home with History*, the former First Lady presented photos and details about living in the White House during the time Bill Clinton was president.

Hillary Clinton also wrote an autobiography titled *Living History*. While the book provides a fresh perspective on Hillary's life with Bill Clinton, it does not go into much detail about the scandals and controversies during Bill's time in the public eye. This may disappoint some readers who are looking for sensationalism, but those who want to know more about Hillary Clinton and the way she views life in general and politics in specific may find it a fascinating read.

In 2015, Hillary Rodham Clinton wrote a book about her tenure as Secretary of State during the Obama Administration in a book titled *Hard Choices.* The book has been widely praised as an intelligent and insightful treatment of U.S. and world issues during that time.

Other writers have written over 50 books about Hillary Clinton. Some of the books are pro-Hillary, while others are against her. However, a good number of them present a balanced view. President Bill Clinton's autobiography, *My Life*, also includes insights into Hillary's actions and character.

# Chapter 14

# U.S. Senator

Hillary Clinton served in the U.S. Senate, representing the state of New York, from 2001 to 2009. There, she served on the Senate budget committee, the armed forces committee, the Committee on Environment and Public Works, the Committee on Health, Education, Labor and Pensions, the Special Committee on Aging and the Commission on Security and Cooperation in Europe.

Senator Clinton supported the war in Iraq, as well as U.S. military involvement in Afghanistan. A part of her stated reason for the Afghanistan decision was that it would improve conditions for Afghani women while fighting back to curb terrorism. In 2005, she spoke out for a middle ground between an abrupt withdrawal of forces and staying "until the job is done," as Bush had stated. More recently, she has commented that her vote for the Iraq War Resolution was wrong and that she had made a mistake in that regard.

In 2007, Clinton opposed an Iraq War troop surge. Later that year, she supported a bill that would reduce funding for the war and demand that Bush withdraw troops by a deadline.

While in the Senate, Senator Clinton sponsored 251 bills. Many of them were written to address issues relating to health care. She sponsored bills on the operation of the government, economics and public finance, science and technology, communications, social welfare, families, education, and labor and employment.

Hillary Clinton has been a supporter of LGBT rights before, during, and after her time in the Senate. While a Senator, she voted against an amendment that would have prohibited same-sex marriage in the U.S. More recently, she supported the cause by participating in the New York Pride parade to support nondiscrimination for the LGBT community.

Clinton contributed to the founding and operation of the Center for American Progress, Citizens for Responsibility and Ethics in Washington, and Media Matters for America. She also won a victory as she convinced Harry Reid to establish a war room for daily Senate communications.

In 2007-2008, the housing bubble had burst and the country was in a financial crisis. Clinton voted in favor of bailing out the nation's financial system.

From 2007 to the end of her second term as Senator in 2009, Hillary Clinton added yet another job for herself. Many American leaders had been saying for years that Hillary might one day be president. In January 2007, she announced that she planned to do just that.

# Chapter 15

# First Presidential Campaign

When Hillary Clinton announced she would run for President of the United States in early 2007, she had already established herself as a tough political opponent. Over two dozen women had run for president before her, but the argument can be made that she broke new ground as the first to be a serious contender. Clinton decided to seize that opportunity and immediately began making preparations for the campaign.

Clinton filed the paperwork and set up an exploratory committee for the campaign. She reportedly gathered a group of celebrities and others with significant fundraising potential, calling them the "Hillraisers," and asked each of these people to raise $1 million in funds for her campaign.

In all, there were over 200 Hillraisers, including celebrities like Magic Johnson, senators like Dianne Feinstein, governors like Pennsylvania governor Ed Rendell, and artists like Stephen Spielberg and John Grisham. Elton John raised $2.5 million with a concert at Radio City Music Hall. Although she managed to raise more funds for her campaign than any past Democrat, she was over $22 million in debt when she left the race.

Several allegations were made about the Clinton fundraising team's methods. For instance, it was alleged that poor Clinton supporters were being pushed to donate over $1000 each. Another allegation was that someone with deep pockets was contributing to the campaign under many different false identities. Although allegations continued to surface, none were ever proven.

In October 2007, an independent study found that Hillary Clinton was getting more media coverage than any other presidential candidate. With 27% of the Clinton stories being positive and 35% being neutral, Clinton developed a strong media presence, although the remaining 38% of the stories were negative. Later that year, the Clinton camp along with media analyst Howard Kurtz said that Obama was getting more than his share of favorable press.

In particular, according to Media Matters, one reporter was over the top in his praise of Obama and his criticisms of Hillary – MSNBC's Chris Matthews. Matthews continued to speak out against Clinton right up through election day. According to a January 2008 poll conducted by New York Times and CBS News, 51% of Democratic voters felt that the media had been more critical of Clinton than of Obama or any other candidate for that matter.

Patti Solis Doyle started as Clinton's campaign manager. In February 2008, Clinton reorganized her team, changing campaign managers to Maggie Williams as well as switching up a few other members of the team.

The primary race was close at several points. Hillary Clinton started strong, but soon Barack Obama closed the gap. When the Super Tuesday results came in, Clinton had won more of the popular votes, but Obama had won more states. When Obama had gained enough pledged and super delegates to win the nomination, Clinton suspended her campaign.

Some pundits said she should have dropped out sooner, while her supporters believed she should fight for the nomination as long as there was any hope of winning it. When she decided it was time to leave, she then endorsed Barack Obama and vowed to work hard to help him win the general election.

By the time Barack Obama had won the presidential election, Hillary Clinton's role in the federal government seemed to be ready to fade dramatically. However, Obama had a surprise waiting for her. He wanted her to be his Secretary of State.

# Chapter 16

# Secretary of State

Shortly after winning the presidential election, Barack Obama met with Hillary Clinton to discuss the possibility that she might accept the position as his Secretary of State. She hesitated at first, wanting to keep her seat in the U.S. Senate, but eventually decided it would be a rewarding challenge to take the State Department position. With a public approval rating of over 65%, Clinton was quickly confirmed as Secretary of State by Congress. She took office on the same day she was confirmed, January 21, 2009.

Clinton spent the first few months getting to know the history, the former Secretaries of State and the issues she would face. She put her former campaign manager Maggie Williams in charge of hiring State Department staffers. She worked with Obama to select several special envoys to go to the world's problem areas on behalf of the U.S.

Hillary's initial goals were to create a stronger State Department with a larger budget to handle international affairs and a more significant role in world economics. She wanted to up the country's diplomatic presence in troubled countries such as Iraq. She also worked toward giving the same attention to aid as to diplomatic missions. She emphasized the need for both diplomacy and development in the world.

Clinton instituted the Quadrennial Diplomacy and Development Review in 2009 to set diplomatic goals for the State Department. She filed her first report, titled *Leading Through Civilian Power*, in 2010. Aside from the goal established in the title, she also emphasized the "Hillary Doctrine," which says that women's issues throughout the world are national security issues in the U.S.

Later in 2009, Clinton introduced the Global Hunger and Food Security Initiative, which is designed to address current and future food shortages using agricultural, nutritional, trade-related, and innovative measures.

Some countries responded to Hillary Clinton's position as Secretary of State by posting a total of 25 female ambassadors to Washington. Clinton specifically budgeted for promoting the best interests of women throughout the world. She also started up the Women in Public Service Project, which she anticipated would bring about gender equality in terms of numbers of public servants of both genders within 40 years.

Clinton worked with U.S. allies to create unification among the Libyan rebels who were in the process of ousting Gaddafi. She often used technology and social media for communications and support in the diplomatic community and to support individuals in conflict with their leaders.

In her many travels as Secretary of State, Clinton enjoyed a certain popularity among local people she visited with and spent time with. She also visited leaders of many countries, including Japan, Indonesia, China, South Korea, Israel, and the NATO meeting of foreign ministers that was held in Brussels.

When she visited Russia, she posed for a photo with their foreign minister, Sergey Lavrov, but the publication of the photo led to a minor misunderstanding. The intent was to show them resetting their relationship after years of disagreements. However, the word used on the photo, "peregruzka," meant "overloaded" rather than "reset." The incident turned into a bit of a joke, which people generally referred to as the Russian reset.

In the Middle East, Clinton wanted to improve conditions for the women of that region. In the 2011 Tohoku earthquake and tsunami, she offered support. She dealt with problems in Haiti, Honduras, Egypt, and Pakistan. Clinton argued and won a debate within the administration to send more troops to Afghanistan.

In 2012, Clinton expressed the desire to move out of the limelight of national politics. She said she would not serve another term as Secretary of State if Obama were re-elected. She eventually agreed to stay until Obama could find a replacement for her and did stay on until 2013.

Overall, Hillary Clinton had enjoyed many successes as Secretary of State. However, on September 11, 2012, she would face an extremely challenging situation. The U.S. diplomatic mission came under attack. With four Americans dead, Secretary Clinton faced a nation that wanted to know why.

# Chapter 17

# Benghazi and Emails

One year to the day after the 9/11 attacks on the Twin Towers of the World Trade Center, another attack happened, this time in Benghazi, Libya. Although the date seems significant, no evidence has been found that it was considered by those who led the attack.

This time, the target was a small diplomatic mission and its nearby security compound. When then-Secretary of State Hillary Clinton found out the attack had gone down and there were American fatalities, she immediately spoke out against the militants at the center of the Battle of Benghazi. Four were dead, including Ambassador J. Christopher Stevens, and three other Americans attached to the mission.

At that point, Clinton had little information about why the consulate was attacked or who was responsible. However, intelligence operatives who had witnessed escalating violence in the area and then the beginning of the attack had called several times asking for more security. Agents at the site alleged that Hillary Clinton was warned of this need but had refused to respond.

Clinton tells a different story. According to the former Secretary of State, other members of the State Department handled the requests and made the decisions. She said that she accepted the responsibility as the leader of the department and deeply regretted the resulting casualties.

Another controversy revolved around the reason for the attack. Initially, some believed that the attack was due to an inflammatory anti-Muslim film that surfaced on the Internet. Others saw the attack as coming from terrorists. Clinton did not jump on either bandwagon right away but emphasized that the most critical task ahead was to find and bring to justice those who had attacked the compound and killed the innocent Americans.

A sound-bite was run on national television which at first seemed to imply that Clinton did not care about the killings in Benghazi. However, the context of the statement was left off the clip. Clinton had been talking about not caring why the event took place at that point but being more concerned about tracking down the militants as soon as possible.

Homeland Security published a report titled "Flashing Red: A Special Report on the Terrorist Attack at Benghazi" that December. The report indicated that there had been a growing risk for Americans in Benghazi since February 2011. During the time between then and the attack, there had been 50 security incidents in Benghazi. The report further said that if the State Department had added security or closed the embassy, either would have been more than justified before the attack.

Senator John McCain called the failure of the State Department to prevent the attacks either "a massive coverup or incompetence" during a Face the Nation broadcast in October. When Mike Rogers, then-committee chair for the Benghazi investigation, read an intelligence report published in 2014, he agreed with McCain's statement.

Obama presented a different view, later suggesting that the Republicans in Congress were chasing "phony scandals" instead of working on the real economic issues that needed to be faced in America.

After several investigations had been held on the Benghazi attacks and Senator Clinton's alleged part in it, she was never found guilty of any wrongdoing.

The controversy first arose in 2015 when the public found out about Clinton's email habits. Rather than using the State Department's secure email servers, Clinton had used a private email server and private email address to conduct government communications. An FBI investigation concluded that 113 emails on Clinton's server contained information that would have been deemed classified at the time it was sent. On July 5, 2016, the FBI recommended dropping all charges, but said that Clinton had been "very careless." On July 7, the State Department reopened its investigation.

# Chapter 18

# Second Presidential Campaign

Hillary Clinton announced on April 12, 2015, that she would run for president in the 2016 election. She had already set the groundwork for her campaign, gathering donors, forming political action committees, and preparing to set up headquarters in Brooklyn. At first, the nomination seemed almost guaranteed to go to Clinton. However, about a month and a half later, another Democratic candidate entered the race.

Bernie Sanders had been a Representative for Vermont and was at that time a U.S. Senator. He told the country he was a democratic socialist, but surprisingly to many conservatives, he achieved a wide following.

Clinton has talked about improving economic conditions for the middle class, instituting preschool for all children in that age range, decreasing the cost of higher education and fine-tuning the Affordable Care Act. She wanted to empower women and enshrine more rights for them. She wanted constitutional amendments to give LGBTQ people the right to marry in same-sex partnerships and to limit political campaigns' ability to take in unaccountable funds. She spoke out against Trump's insistence that Muslims should be banned from the United States.

She wanted to work toward equal pay for equal work. Clinton also said that undocumented immigrants need to have a defined path to citizenship.

Clinton barely won the Iowa caucuses, but Sanders won the first primary held in New Hampshire. On Super Tuesday, Hillary Clinton pulled ahead with 7 of the 11 primaries, primarily aided by Southern Democrats. Still, the primary race was relatively close, with Sanders receiving 13 million votes to Clinton's 17 million.

Sanders was been slow to drop out, but Clinton won the nomination of the Democratic Party at their convention on July 26, 2016. She chose Senator Time Kaine as her running mate, and he was nominated the next day.

Donald Trump easily emerged from the Republican primaries to be Clinton's Republican opponent heading into the general election. Clinton and Trump each took small leads in the polls after their respective parties held their national conventions, but on Election Day, November 8, 2016, Donald Trump emerged the winner.

# Conclusion

On January 20, 2017, while attending the inauguration of Donald Trump with her husband and daughter, Hillary Clinton tweeted, "I'm here today to honor our democracy & its enduring values, I will never stop believing in our country & its future."

In the years that followed the 2016 election, Clinton received honorary doctorates degrees, embarked on speaking tours, announced the formation of a new political action committee, wrote best-selling books, was appointed Chancellor of Queen's University in Belfast, and endorsed Joe Biden for President in the 2020 election,

Hillary Rodham Clinton has led a fascinating and accomplished life. Although not everyone would agree with her methods, she is a renowned policy wonk and has worked within the system to try and improve the world and the lives of her constituents. Expect to hear more from and about Hillary Rodham Clinton for many more years.

Printed in Great Britain
by Amazon